NOT-SO-ORDINARY SCIENCE

GET MOVING WITH SCIENCE!

PROJECTS THAT ZOOM, FLY, AND MORE

by Elsie Olson

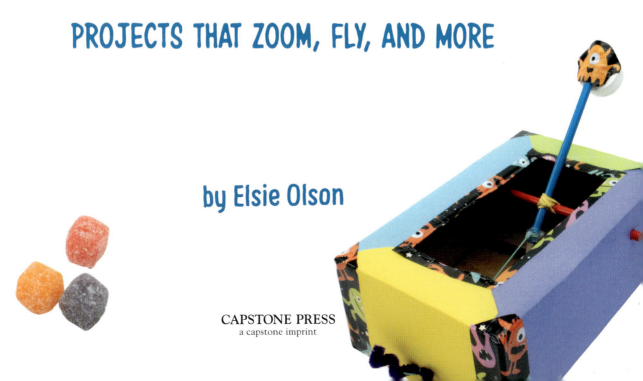

CAPSTONE PRESS
a capstone imprint

Dabble Lab is published by Capstone Press, an imprint of Capstone.
1710 Roe Crest Drive, North Mankato, Minnesota 56003
capstonepub.com

Copyright © 2023 by Capstone. All rights reserved. No part of this publication
may be reproduced in whole or in part, or stored in a retrieval system, or
transmitted in any form or by any means, electronic, mechanical, photocopying,
recording, or otherwise, without written permission of the publisher.

**Library of Congress Cataloging-in-Publication Data is available on the Library
of Congress website.**
ISBN: 9781666342321 (hardcover)
ISBN: 9781666342338 (ebook PDF)

Summary: Do you like to get moving? These science projects are for you! Make
tiny buzzing robots out of toothbrush heads. Build a catapult that shoots candy.
Then, learn the science behind each moving part!

Image Credits
Shutterstock: ONYXprj (background), Front Cover, Back Cover, alarich, 4
(yarn), Aleksandr178 (wire stripper), 4, 20, andRiU92, 4 (batteries), arsslawa
(rubber bands), Natakorn Ruangrit (scissors), 4, 18, Paul Orr (hole punch), 4, 24,
PrimaStockPhoto (ruler), 4, 18, Rok Breznik (motor), 4, 20, Sergei Bogachov (glue
gun), 4, 14, Mona Makela, 6 (iron oxide), Purple Clouds, 6 (black slime), Ricardo
Javier, 6 (magnets), SweetLemons, 20 (googly eyes), optimarc, 22 (chenille stems),
Denis Dryashkin, 26 (nail), Svitlana Martynova, 26 (paint and paintbrushes),
showcake, 27 (fan), OttoPles, 28 (tape), Craig Walton, 31 (magnets)

Design Elements
Shutterstock: MicroOne (gauges)
All project photos shot by Mighty Media, Inc.

Editorial Credits
Editor: Jessica Rusick
Designer: Aruna Rangarajan

All internet sites appearing in back matter were available and accurate when this
book was sent to press.

The publisher and the author shall not be liable for any damages allegedly
arising from the information in this book, and they specifically disclaim any
liability from the use or application of any of the contents of this book.

TABLE OF CONTENTS

Make It Move!	4
Slithering Slime	6
Super Sailboat	8
Candy Catapult	10
Rubber Band Truck	14
Zoom Bottle Blastoff	18
Whirling Frog	20
Buzzing Bug Bots	22
Twirling Rainbow	24
Whirring Windmill	26
Floating Train	28
Read More	32
Internet Sites	32

MAKE IT MOVE!

What happens when forces make things fly, creep, and zoom? It turns out motion science projects also happen to be fantastically fun. So grab your stopwatch, put on your lab coat, and prepare to duck.

THINGS ARE ABOUT TO GET MOVING!

GENERAL SUPPLIES & TOOLS

batteries · duct tape · hole punch · hot glue gun · mini motors

rubber bands · ruler · scissors · string · wire stripper

TIPS & TRICKS

FOLLOW THESE SIMPLE TIPS TO STAY SAFE AND HAVE FUN!

- **Read all the steps** and gather all your supplies before starting a project.

- **Wash your hands** after handling slime.

- **Some of these projects involve flying objects.** Be sure your work area is large enough so projects don't cause injury or damage.

- **Ask an adult** to help when using hot or sharp tools.

- **Mini motors, magnets, and many other materials** in this book can be purchased at hardware stores or online.

SCIENCE TERMS TO KNOW

CENTRIFUGAL FORCE (sen-TRI-fuh-guhl FORS): a force that causes an object moving in a circular path to move out and away from the center of its path

CIRCUIT (SUHR-kuht): the complete path that an electric current travels along

FORCE (FORS): a physical power, such as gravity, that can affect the movement of an object

FRICTION (FRIK-shuhn): the force that causes a moving object to slow down when it is touching another object

MAGNETISM (MAG-neh-ti-zem): a magnet's power to attract or repel certain metals and other magnets

SLITHERING SLIME

Magnets can make objects move. Use the force of magnetism to cause slime to **creep across a table!**

WHAT YOU NEED

- ⅓ cup (79 milliliters) school glue
- 3 tablespoons (44 mL) iron oxide powder
- mixing bowl & spoon
- ¼ cup (59 mL) liquid starch
- rubber or latex gloves
- neodymium magnets

WHAT YOU DO

STEP 1
Mix the school glue and iron oxide powder together in a bowl.

STEP 2
Add the liquid starch to the school glue and iron oxide mixture. Stir until the mixture begins to thicken.

STEP 3
Put on gloves. Mix the slime with your hands until it is no longer sticky.

STEP 4
Put the slime on your work surface. Set a magnet near the slime. Watch the slime move!

WHAT YOU GET

Magnetism! Magnetism is a force that makes certain metals move toward each other. Iron is a metal. So is the neodymium magnet. Magnets are surrounded by a magnetic field. When slime enters the field, the iron oxide is pulled toward the magnet. **That's science!**

SUPER SAILBOAT

Build a plastic bottle boat and use electricity to send it zipping **across the water!**

WHAT YOU NEED

- plastic water bottle
- craft knife
- battery holder & batteries
- wire stripper
- motorized micro propeller
- electrical tape
- art supplies
- tub or sink filled with water

▲ ▲ ▲
EXPERIMENT!
WHAT ELSE COULD YOU USE FOR THE HULLS? IS THERE A BETTER PLACE TO PUT THE BATTERY HOLDER?
▼ ▼ ▼

WHAT YOU DO

STEP 1

Cut the neck off the bottle. Cut the bottle in half lengthwise. These are the boat's hulls.

STEP 2
Strip the coating off the ends of the battery holder's wires. Wrap the ends around the connectors on the motor.

STEP 3

Tape the motor between the hulls so the post sticks out behind the boat. Tape the battery holder inside one hull.

STEP 4
Decorate the boat if you'd like. Put the propeller on the motor. Set the boat in water. Make sure the propeller is in the water and the motor is not. Turn on the motor and watch your boat go!

WHAT YOU GET

The power of electricity! Connecting the wires from the batteries to the motor completes a circuit. The circuit lets electricity flow from the batteries to the motor and back. This electricity powers the motor and turns the propeller. **That's science!**

CANDY CATAPULT

Study forces and motion by launching objects with a mini catapult. **You can make candy fly!**

WHAT YOU NEED

- shoebox
- scissors
- ruler
- art supplies
- pushpin
- 2 pencils longer than the box's width
- 2 rubber bands
- hot glue gun
- chenille stem
- plastic bottle cap
- gumdrops or other small candies

10

WHAT YOU DO

STEP 1
Cut a large rectangular hole in the shoebox's lid. Leave about 1 inch (2.5 centimeters) at each end. Tape the lid in place if necessary. Decorate the shoebox.

STEP 2
Poke a pushpin into one long side of the box, about ½ inch (1.2 cm) from the top and 3 inches (8 cm) from one end.

STEP 3
Push a pencil through the hole to the other side of the box. Poke a hole in that side for the pencil to go through.

STEP 4
Use a rubber band to secure the second pencil to the middle of the first in a cross shape. About 2 inches (5 cm) of the second pencil should stick down below the first pencil.

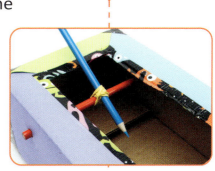

Continued on the next page.

11

STEP 5

Cut the second rubber band. Tie one end to the second pencil below the first pencil. Hot glue can help hold the rubber band in place.

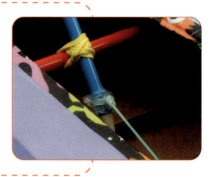

STEP 6

In the end of the box opposite the pencils, poke a hole 1 inch (2.5 cm) up from the bottom.

STEP 7

String the loose end of the cut rubber band through the hole. Pull until the rubber band is tight. Tie the end around a small piece of chenille stem.

STEP 8

Hot glue a plastic bottle cap to the top of the second pencil. The inside of the cap should face away from the stretched rubber band.

STEP 9

Pull the end of the pencil with the cap down toward the box. Set a piece of candy in the cap. Let go and watch the candy fly!

EXPERIMENT! TRY USING DIFFERENT TYPES OF CANDY AND OTHER OBJECTS. WHICH FLIES THE FARTHEST?

WHAT YOU GET

Energy transfer! Every object has potential energy. This means it could move in the right conditions. Moving objects have kinetic energy. When you pull the pencil down, the rubber band has potential energy. When you let go, kinetic energy from the rubber band transfers to the object, shooting it through the air. The object has kinetic energy while it is flying. **That's science!**

RUBBER BAND TRUCK

This monster truck doesn't need fuel to go. **It's powered by a rubber band!**

WHAT YOU NEED

- cardboard box
- art supplies
- 2 wooden skewers
- ruler
- pencil
- drinking straws
- scissors
- hot glue gun
- rubber band
- paper clip
- 4 empty tape tubes
- cardboard
- duct tape
- pushpin
- small box (optional)

WHAT YOU DO

STEP 1

Decorate the cardboard box. This will be the body of your truck. Make sure you can still access the inside of the box.

STEP 2
Use a wooden skewer to poke two holes through one long side of the box. The holes should be about 1 inch (2.5 cm) from each end. Poke two holes through the box's other side. Make sure the holes line up with those on the first side.

STEP 3

Use a pencil to make the holes big enough for the straws to fit through. Cut four straw pieces that are each about 2 inches (5 cm) long. Push a straw piece through each hole. Use hot glue to hold them in place.

STEP 4
Slide a wooden skewer through each pair of straws. These are the truck's axles.

Continued on the next page.

15

STEP 5

Loop a rubber band around one skewer. Loop the other end of the rubber band around a paper clip. Attach the paper clip to the closest short end of the box. Close the box lid and secure it shut.

STEP 6

Trace the inside of a tape tube four times on cardboard. Cut out the circles. Decorate them if you like.

STEP 7

Wrap each tape tube in duct tape. Fit a cardboard circle inside each tube. Trim the circles if necessary and glue them in place. These are the truck's wheels.

STEP 8

Use a pushpin to poke a hole in the center of each wheel. Use a pencil to make the holes big enough for the skewers to fit through. Push each wheel onto the end of a skewer.

STEP 9

If you'd like, decorate a second, smaller box. Add it to the top of your truck to make the cab.

STEP 10

Set the truck on an even surface. Roll it backward until the wheels won't turn anymore. Let go of the truck. Watch it zoom away!

WHAT YOU GET

Elastic action! Rubber bands are elastic. This means they stretch when pulled. Stretched rubber bands store potential energy. Pulling the truck back causes the rubber band to wrap around the axle and stretch. When you let the truck go, the rubber band snaps back in place, converting the potential energy into kinetic energy. This energy makes the truck go! **That's science!**

ZOOM BOTTLE BLASTOFF

Harness the power of inertia to make your own zoom bottle. **How fast can you make it zip?**

WHAT YOU NEED

- 2 water bottles
- scissors
- tape
- string
- ruler
- art supplies
- partner

EXPERIMENT!
WHAT HAPPENS IF YOU CHANGE THE LENGTH OF THE STRINGS? OR IF ONE PERSON RAISES THEIR END HIGHER?

WHAT YOU DO

STEP 1
Cut the top half off each bottle. Tape them together at the center.

STEP 2
Cut two pieces of string 10 to 12 feet (3 to 4 meters) long. Tie a large loop in each end of both strings. Thread the strings through the bottle. Decorate the bottle.

STEP 3
Hold the loops on one side. Hold one loop in each hand. Have a partner hold the loops on the other side. Back away from each other until the strings are tight.

STEP 4
The person nearest the bottle should snap their strings apart. The bottle will zoom away! Have the other person bring their strings together as the bottle comes near. Then they can snap their strings apart to send the bottle back. Keep blasting the bottle back and forth!

WHAT YOU GET

Inertia in action! Objects don't move unless a force makes them. They then keep moving until a new force stops them. This concept is called inertia. Separating the strings creates a force that sends the bottle shooting forward. When the other person separates their strings, that force sends the bottle zooming in the other direction. **That's science!**

WHIRLING FROG

Use electricity and force to create a friendly frog that **whirls, shakes, and jitters!**

WHAT YOU NEED

- AAA battery holder with switch & batteries
- wire stripper
- 1.5–3 V mini motor
- pencil with eraser
- scissors
- CD
- hot glue gun
- duct tape
- craft foam
- googly eyes
- markers

20

WHAT YOU DO

STEP 1
Strip the coating off the ends of the battery holder's wires. Wrap the ends around the connectors on the motor.

STEP 2
Cut the eraser off a pencil. Press the eraser onto the motor's post.

STEP 3
Set the motor on the CD so the eraser sticks through the hole. Hot glue the motor in place.

STEP 4
Tape the battery holder next to the motor on the CD. Cover the CD with duct tape.

STEP 5
Cut a frog out of craft foam. Use googly eyes, tape, and markers to add details.

STEP 6
Hot glue the bottom edge of the frog to the CD. Let the glue dry. Set the frog on a hard floor. Turn on the motor. Watch the frog spin!

WHAT YOU GET

Friction! Friction is a force that acts between two objects rubbing against each other. When the motor is turned on, the eraser rubs against the floor. The friction between the eraser and the floor makes the frog jump and turn. **That's science!**

BUZZING BUG BOTS

Construct a swarm of robot bugs. **They'll create a lot of buzz!**

WHAT YOU NEED

- toothbrushes with flat bristles
- tin snips
- mini vibrating motors with wires
- wire stripper
- hot glue gun
- button batteries
- tape
- chenille stems
- scissors
- googly eyes

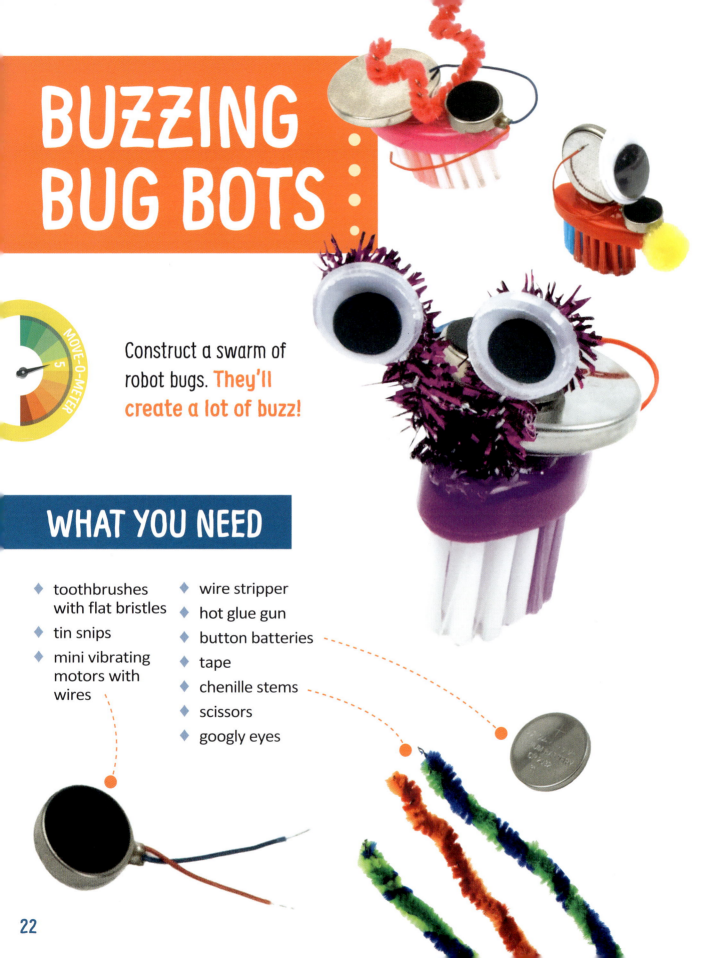

22

WHAT YOU DO

STEP 1

Use tin snips to cut the head off a toothbrush. Strip the coating off the ends of a motor's wires.

STEP 2

Glue the motor to the top of a battery. Glue the bottom of the battery to the toothbrush head.

STEP 3

Tape one of the wires to the bottom of the battery. Cut a short piece of chenille stem. Fold it into a V shape. Glue the chenille stem to the front of the toothbrush head. Glue googly eyes to the chenille stem.

STEP 4

When your swarm is ready, set the bots on a hard, flat surface. Tape the top wires to the batteries. Watch your bots buzz!

Repeat **steps 1 through 3** to make more bug bots.

WHAT YOU GET

Circuits and friction! The wires form a circuit that lets electricity flow between the battery and the motor. This electricity makes the bot vibrate. The vibrations create friction between the bristles and the flat surface. This friction propels the bots across the surface. **That's science!**

23

TWIRLING RAINBOW

Colors are on the move with this spinner! Twirl the dowel and watch the rainbow **expand and contract.**

WHAT YOU NEED

- paper in six colors
- scissors
- ruler
- hole punch
- wooden dowel
- pushpin

EXPERIMENT!
WHAT HAPPENS TO THE STRIPS OF PAPER WHEN YOU SPIN THE DOWEL FASTER? WHAT HAPPENS IF YOU USE LONGER STRIPS OF PAPER?

WHAT YOU DO

STEP 1
Cut two strips of each color paper. Make each strip 1¼ by 11 inches (3 by 28 cm).

STEP 2
Punch a hole near one end of each strip. Make sure the dowel fits easily through the holes.

STEP 3
Stack the strips in rainbow order. Line up the holes. Push the dowel through them. Pin the strips to the top of the dowel.

STEP 4
Fan out the strips to form a ball. Rotate the dowel and watch the colors spin!

WHAT YOU GET

Centrifugal force! This force causes a rotating object to move away from the center of its rotation. The dowel is the center of rotation. When you rotate the dowel, centrifugal force pushes the strips of paper out to form a wider, flatter ball. **That's science!**

WHIRRING WINDMILL

Build a simple and sleek windmill to harness the **power of the wind.**

WHAT YOU NEED

- 19 large craft sticks
- hot glue gun
- paper towel tube
- large nail with a flat head
- small rubber band
- ruler
- scissors
- plastic bottle cap
- paint & paintbrushes
- electric fan

26

WHAT YOU DO

STEP 1
Lay eight craft sticks side by side. Glue eight sticks side by side across them. This forms a square base for the windmill.

STEP 2
Hot glue the paper towel tube to the middle of the base. Make sure it's secure.

STEP 3
Wrap a rubber band around a nail about ⅓ inch (1 cm) from the head. Poke the nail through the tube 1 inch (2.5 cm) from the top.

STEP 4
Cut the remaining three craft sticks in half. Hot glue the stick halves around a bottle cap so they are all slightly angled in the same direction.

STEP 5
Hot glue the nail's head to the inside of the bottle cap. Paint your windmill. Set your windmill in front of a fan. Does the windmill turn?

WHAT YOU GET

Wind power! The wind from the fan blows on the windmill blades. Because the blades are angled, the force of the wind pushes them sideways. This makes the windmill turn. **That's science!**

27

FLOATING TRAIN

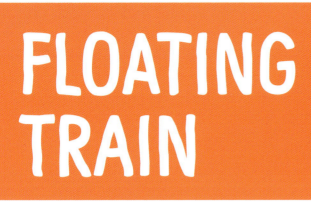

Make your own train that hovers above the tracks. What's behind the magical motion? **Magnets!**

WHAT YOU NEED

- monopolar magnetic tape
- whiteboard eraser
- scissors
- ruler
- toilet paper tube
- glue
- art supplies
- black paper
- white tissue paper
- cardboard

WHAT YOU DO

STEP 1
Stick two strips of magnetic tape to the back of the whiteboard eraser. There should be ½ inch (1.2 cm) between the strips.

STEP 2
Cut the toilet paper tube lengthwise. Glue the edges to the sides of the eraser to form the train's body. Decorate the train.

STEP 3
Make a smokestack for the top of the train. Roll a small piece of black paper into a tube. Glue tissue paper on top. Glue the smokestack to the train.

STEP 4
Cut three strips of cardboard that are about 2 feet (0.6 m) long and 3½ inches (9 cm) wide.

Continued on the next page.

STEP 5

Draw two straight lines on a cardboard strip 1½ inches (4 cm) from each long side.

STEP 6

Stick two strips of magnetic tape on the cardboard strip. Line the tape up outside the pencil lines so there is ½ inch (1.2 cm) between the magnets.

STEP 7

Fold the remaining cardboard strips lengthwise so each fold is 1 inch (2.5 cm) from one side.

STEP 8

Place the thinner flaps of the folded cardboard strips on the first strip. Line them up so the folded edges are parallel to the magnets. Glue down the thin flaps. The wider flaps should stick up straight.

STEP 9
Place the train on the track.
Push it gently and watch it float!

EXPERIMENT! TRY ADDING EXTRA WEIGHT TO YOUR TRAIN CAR. DOES IT STILL FLOAT?

WHAT YOU GET

Magnetic levitation! Magnets have two poles. One side is the north pole. The other side is the south pole. When matching poles of two magnets face one another, the magnets push apart. This force causes the train to hover. **That's science!**

READ MORE

Borgert-Spaniol, Megan. *Build a Roller Coaster! And More Engineering Challenges.* Minneapolis: Abdo Publishing, 2021.

Smibert, Angie. *Fairground Physics: Motion, Momentum, and Magnets with Hands-On Science Activities.* Norwich, VT: Nomad Press, 2020.

Ventura, Marne. *Motion Projects to Build On.* North Mankato, MN: Capstone Press, 2019.

INTERNET SITES

DK Find Out!—Forces and Motion
dkfindout.com/us/science/forces-and-motion

PBS Science Trek—Force and Motion
pbs.org/video/science-trek-force-and-motion

Sciencing—Fun Science Activities for Force & Motion
sciencing.com/fun-science-activities-for-force-motion-12744481.html

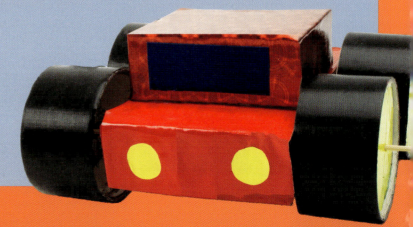